Little Bunny's Book of Thoughts

Little Bunny's Book of Thoughts
Published in Great Britain in 2020 by Graffeg Limited.

Second Edition 2021

Written and illustrated by Steve Smallman copyright
© 2020. Designed and produced by Graffeg Limited
copyright © 2020.

Graffeg Limited, 24 Stradey Park Business Centre,
Mwrwg Road, Llangennech, Llanelli, Carmarthenshire,
SA14 8YP, Wales, UK. Tel: 01554 824000.
www.graffeg.com.

Steve Smallman is hereby identified as the author
of this work in accordance with section 77 of the
Copyrights, Designs and Patents Act 1988.

A CIP Catalogue record for this book is
available from the British Library.

ISBN 9781913134259

2 3 4 5 6 7 8 9

MIX
Paper from
responsible sources
FSC® C014138

Little Bunny's Book of Thoughts

Steve Smallman

This book belongs to:

_____

_____

_____

GRAFFEG

When everything seems to be
just out of reach

You feel lost and alone, all at sea.

When you're looking for something

But not really sure anymore what that something might be.

When life seems to be
such a struggle
And everything gets
in your way

When nothing goes right
And it looks like it might...

Turn into an 'ears-down day'.

Just stop.

Don't be swamped by your
worries and fears,
Open your eyes,
and lift up your ears!

Try looking at life from a new, different angle

Hang upside down and
let your ears dangle!

Look all around, that's
the way to begin,

You'll see so much more
looking out and not 'in'.

Meet up with friends,
stop and talk for a while,

And in no time at all you'll
remember to smile!

And you'll start to feel good and
you'll see that it's daft
That it's such a long time since
you last really laughed.

So relax, cool your ears,
just lie back and chill,
Be kind to yourself
if no one else will.

Dare to believe that a wish
can come true,

That something amazing
is waiting for you!

And knowing that life's
not as bad as it seems,

You'll sleep tight, all night,
and dream sweet dreams.

Steve Smallman

Steve Smallman has been writing and illustrating children's books for over 40 years. The author of *Smelly Peter the Great Pea Eater* (winner of the Sheffield Children's Book Award 2009) and *The Lamb Who Came for Dinner* (shortlisted for the Red House Children's Book Award and read by Meatloaf on CITV's *Bookaboo*), he received the Sheffield Children's Book Award again in 2019 for *Cock-a-Doodle Poo!*. Steve started working as an illustrator while he was still at art college, then, after about 20 years, decided to have a go at writing stories of his own. He has so far written over 100 books, with more on the way.

'*Little Bunny's Book of Thoughts* started with a doodle in my sketchbook. I was trying out a different technique using a soft pencil on a grainy textured paper. Without much conscious thought on my part, a worried little bunny appeared in a makeshift boat. I posted the drawing on social media and it seemed to strike a chord with so many people! So I drew more bunny pictures using different facial expressions and scenarios and soon had quite a collection. Put together they seemed to show an emotional journey for the little bunny that people could relate to. I added a minimal text to help bunny on his way and with the help of Graffeg, this book was born!'

Graffeg Children's Books

The White Hare
Nicola Davies
Illustrated by Anastasia Izlesou

Mother Cary's Butter Knife
Nicola Davies
Illustrated by Anja Uhren

Elias Martin
Nicola Davies
Illustrated by Fran Shum

The Selkie's Mate
Nicola Davies
Illustrated by Claire Jenkins

Bee Boy and the Moonflowers
Nicola Davies
Illustrated by Max Low

The Eel Question
Nicola Davies
Illustrated by Beth Holland

Perfect
Nicola Davies
Illustrated by Cathy Fisher

The Pond
Nicola Davies
Illustrated by Cathy Fisher

The Quiet Music of Gently Falling Snow
Jackie Morris

The Ice Bear
Jackie Morris

The Snow Leopard
Jackie Morris

Queen of the Sky
Jackie Morris

Through the Eyes of Me
Jon Roberts
Illustrated by Hannah Rounding

Through the Eyes of Us
Jon Roberts
Illustrated by Hannah Rounding

Animal Surprises
Nicola Davies
Illustrated by Abbie Cameron

The Word Bird
Nicola Davies
Illustrated by Abbie Cameron

Into the Blue
Nicola Davies
Illustrated by Abbie Cameron

The Secret of the Egg
Nicola Davies
Illustrated by Abbie Cameron

Mouse & Mole series
Joyce Dunbar
Illustrated by James Mayhew
Mouse & Mole
Happy Days for Mouse & Mole
A Very Special Mouse & Mole
Mouse & Mole Have a Party
Mouse & Mole – A Fresh Start

Koshka's Tales – Stories
from Russia
James Mayhew

Leap, Hare, Leap!
Dom Conlon
Illustrated by Anastasia Izlesou

Walking with Bamps
Roy Noble
Illustrated by Karl Davies

The B Team
Roy Noble
Illustrated by Karl Davies

Gaspard the Fox
Zeb Soanes
Illustrated by James Mayhew

Gaspard – Best in Show
Zeb Soanes
Illustrated by James Mayhew

Gaspard's Foxtrot
Zeb Soanes
Illustrated by James Mayhew

Ceri & Deri Series
Max Low
Build a Birdhouse
The Treasure Map
No Time for Clocks
Good to Be Sweet
Young Whippersnapper
The Very Smelly Telly Show

Paradise Found
John Milton
Illustrated by Helen Elliott

Only One of Me – Mum
Lisa Wells and Michelle Robinson
Illustrated by Catalina Echeverri

Only One of Me – Dad
Lisa Wells and Michelle Robinson
Illustrated by Tim Budgen

A Cuddle and a Cwtch
Sarah KilBride
Illustrated by James Munro